Secret Agent

Interactive Quiz

Managing Editors: Simon Melhuish and Sarah Wells
Series Editor: Nikole G Bamford
Designer: Linley J Clode
Writer: Gavin Webster

Published by
The Lagoon Group
PO Box 311, KT2 5QW, UK
PO Box 990676, Boston, MA 02199, USA

ISBN: 1904797199

www.thelagoongroup.com

Printed in China

Secret Agent

Interactive Quiz

IntelliQuest

Instructions

First of all make sure you have a Quizmo —

Find the book's unique code (this appears at the top of this page). Use the ◀ and ▶ buttons to scroll to this number on the Quizmo screen. Press the ⬦ button to enter the code, and you're ready to go.

Use the ◀ ▶ scroll buttons to select the question number you want to answer. Press the **A**, **B**, **C**, or **D** button to enter your chosen answer.

If you are correct the green light beside the button you pressed will flash. You can then use the scroll button to move on to another question.

If your answer is incorrect, the red light beside the button you pressed will flash.

Don't worry, you can try again and again until you have the correct answer, OR move on to another question. (Beware: the more times you guess incorrectly, the lower your final percentage score will be!)

You can finish the quiz at any point — just press the ◆ button to find out your score and rank as follows:

75% or above	Hey there, 007 – secret agent of the century!
50% — 74%	An undercover agent in the making!
25% — 49%	Sorry, you're not quite James Bond yet...
Less than 25%	You need to go undercover – and stay there!

If you do press the ◆ button to find out your score, this will end your session and you will have to use the ◆ to start again!

HAVE FUN!

001

The making and breaking of codes is called...?

- **A** Codeology
- **B** Cipherography
- **C** Cryptography
- **D** Signology

002

The earliest known use of cryptography comes from...?

- **A** Babylon
- **B** Ancient Rome
- **C** Ancient Greece
- **D** Ancient Egypt

003

What was the name of the encrypting device used by the Germans during the Second World War?

- **A** Enigma
- **B** Medusa
- **C** Metropolis
- **D** Electra

Codes

The code was cracked by a section of British intelligence based where?

A Blenheim Palace

B Salisbury

C Cheltenham

D Bletchley Park

During the Second World War, the USA tried to foil eavesdropping Japaneses spies by using which group of people to transmit secret messages?

A New York cab drivers

B Samoans

C Navajo Indians

D Creoles from New Orleans

Before the First World War only three countries had full-time code-breaking departments. Which of the following wasn't one of them?

A Russia

B France

C Austria-Hungary

D Britain

007

What is the difference between code and cipher?

- **A** There's no difference
- **B** Code substitutes individual letters for other letters; cipher substitutes whole words
- **C** Cipher substitutes individual letters for other letters; code substitutes whole words
- **D** Codes are used to signal, ciphers for secret messages

008

What is a Dog Code?

- **A** A code within a code
- **B** A non-written code transmitted in pulses
- **C** A fake code that makes no sense
- **D** An ally's code

009

What name did the Americans give to the cipher machine used by the Japanese during the Second World War?

- **A** Orange
- **B** Deep Blue
- **C** Purple
- **D** Rainbow

Codes

GET CRACKING — CIPHERS TO BE DECIPHERED

Can you decipher the intercepted encrypted messages and answer the question below each one?

emases si drowssap eht

What's the password?

- **A** Steven
- **B** Master
- **C** Sesame
- **D** Superb

XNTQ BNMSZBS VHKK AD
VDZQHMF Z LZTUD SHF

What color are you looking out for?

- **A** Green
- **B** Black
- **C** Brown
- **D** Mauve

25 18 14 9 18/7 21 18/26 22 16 15 2
19 22 25 26/22 1/7 21 18/17 18 14 17/17
5 2 3/2 1/6 8 1 17 14 12

When do you make contact?

- **A** Sunday
- **B** Saturday
- **C** Friday
- **D** Monday

013

45 11 31 15/45 23 15/21 24 43 44 45/11 52 11 24
32 11 12 32 15/21 32 24 22 45/45 35/22 15 34 15
52 11/11 34 14/44 45 11 54/11 45/45 23 15/51 44
51 11 32/41 32 11 13 15. 21 24 43 15 21 32
54/53 24 32 32/13 35 34 45 11 13 45/54 35 51.

Where are you going?

- **A** Warsaw
- **B** Geneva
- **C** Berlin
- **D** Ulan Bator

014

JR WR WKH VDIHKRXVH LQ FURPZHOO URDG
DQG ZDLW IRU LQVWUXFWLRXW

Where is the safehouse?

- **A** Hadrian's Road
- **B** Cromwell Road
- **C** Primrose Road
- **D** Ashburne Road

015

q w7853 yqw g33h 43w34f3e r94 697
q5 5y3 y8o59h 7he34 5y3 hqj3 9r wj65y3.

What is your alias?

- **A** Waters
- **B** Smythe
- **C** MacKay
- **D** Crosby

Equipment & Gadgets

A bug is a listening device which allows a spy to eavesdrop on conversations and telephone calls. There are five types of bug. Which of the following isn't one of them?

A Acoustic
B Ultrasonic
C Optical
D Ultraviolet

Bugs can generally only be detected...?

A When they are installed
B When they get hot
C When they are transmitting
D When they stop working

How do simple telephone bug deactivators work?

A Make the bug run out of tape
B Make the bug explode
C Reroute your conversations, bypassing the bug
D Jam the signal the bug sends back to the eavesdropper

019

The Americans placed a listening device outside a Soviet military base disguised as a what?

- **A** Woodpecker
- **B** Large mushroom
- **C** Tree stump
- **D** Litter bin

020

The Great Seal was a gift from the Russians and hung on the wall of the US embassy in Moscow. Inside was an ingenious listening device known as 'The Thing'. It was very hard to detect because...?

- **A** It had no batteries
- **B** It had no power supply
- **C** It did not transmit radio waves
- **D** All of the above

021

Which of these was a deadly weapon used by the KGB in the cold war?

- **A** Cigarette case gun
- **B** Pair of 1950s dark glasses
- **C** 1950s men's wristwatch
- **D** Packet of chewing gum

Equipment & Gadgets

Silencers work by suppressing the gases that leave the gun barrel when the gun is fired. Which of the following isn't true of silencers?

- **A** They hide the bright muzzle flash of a firing gun
- **B** They use special bullets
- **C** They reduce the effective range of the gun
- **D** They are silent

What is distinctive about the special bullets used with silencers?

- **A** They are lighter
- **B** They travel more slowly
- **C** They are smaller
- **D** They have a special tip

What advantage do revolvers have over other pistols?

- **A** You can modify the bullets
- **B** They are more accurate
- **C** They are quick to draw
- **D** They are lighter

025 When was the microdot (miniature photograph of a document) first used?

A 1812
B 1938
C 1914
D 1852

026 Which of the following gadgets can still only be found on the pages of spy novels?

A Blue X-ray glasses
B Miniature ring camera
C Cigarette lighter communicator
D Satellite phone

027 One of the latest ideas for identifying people is facial thermography in which the characteristic heat patterns emitted by the face are measured. The latest systems can identify individuals regardless of facial hair or even cosmetic surgery by measuring 65,000 different temperature points on the face with an accuracy surpassing that of fingerprints. However, thermographs can be radically changed by what?

A Snow
B Heat wave
C Alcohol consumption
D Wearing a hat

Equipment & Gadgets

A standard weapon for commandoes and spies during and after the Second World War, the Fairbairn-Sykes, fighting knife was designed by two British officers and based on their experience of close-quarters combat with the Shanghai police. What was it specifically designed for?

- **A** Striking accurately at the target's vital organs
- **B** Being light and easy to carry and conceal
- **C** Throwing
- **D** Parrying

In 1984, it was found that an unsecured shipment of office equipment for the US embassy in Moscow had been bugged and had transmitted intelligence data for years. Of what did the office equipment consist?

- **A** Pencils
- **B** Personal computers
- **C** Photocopiers
- **D** Typewriters

Which of the following apparently innocent objects held a deadly weapon and was issued to KGB agents?

- **A** Lipstick gun
- **B** Compact with mirror, face powder, etc
- **C** Mascara brush
- **D** Hairbrush

031

The SR-71 spy plane held the records for speed and altitude for most of the 24 years it was used for surveillance by the Americans. It could fly three and a half times faster than the speed of sound and reach an altitude of 85,000 feet. What was its nickname?

A Eagle

B Condor

C Blackbird

D Albatross

032

Bulgarian dissident Georgi Markov was assassinated by the Bulgarian secret service in London on 7 September 1978 while waiting for a bus. The Bulgarians were provided with a choice of weapons by the KGB. What did they use to kill Markov?

A Umbrella that fired poison pellets

B Gun disguised as a camera

C Exploding bouquet of flowers

D Poisoned chocolate

033

Which of the following was actually used by Soviet agents during the Cold War?

A Hat gun

B Fingernail radio

C Shoe transmitter

D Monocle camera

The world's first satellite surveillance system was called Corona. Each image it sent back to Earth covered an area 10 miles wide and 120 miles long. It could identify objects as small as 2 meters in length. Which country developed and used Corona?

A France
B Soviet Union
C China
D USA

The Russian AK-47 assault rifle is popular around the world. It is estimated that there are between 30 and 50 million of these rifles in the world. What does the 47 stand for?

A Caliber
B First year of manufacture
C Weight
D Forty-seventh version of the weapon

Which of the following is not a characteristic of the AK-47 assault rifle?

A Cheap
B Accurate up to 2500 meters
C Easy to maintain
D Reliable

037

The UZI, designed by Israeli major Uziel Gal, is a favorite of the American secret service because of its small size and high rate of fire. How many rounds per minute does the 9mm version fire?

A 200

B 400

C 600

D 800

038

The principle at work in body armor is quite simple. The material at the heart of a bullet-proof vest is nothing more than...?

A A hard plate

B A deflecting mirror

C Sand

D A very strong net

039

TEMPEST systems are used by spies to do what?

A Listen in on conversations

B Read computer screens

C Communicate covertly

D Interrogate suspects

Fictional Spies

The character of James Bond was created by which novelist?

A Frederick Forsyth

B John le Carre

C Ian Fleming

D G K Chesterton

Bond entered MI6 after World War II and received his license to kill in 1950. During the war he served in...?

A The army

B The airforce

C The navy

D The police

Prior to becoming a best-selling novelist, old Etonian Fleming worked as...?

A A journalist

B A stockbroker

C An intelligence operative

D All of the above

043

Somewhat of an homme fatale, Bond is generally surrounded by beautiful women hanging on his every word. One of the most famous was Honey Ryder, played by Ursula Andress. In which film did she appear?

A Dr No

B From Russia With Love

C You Only Live Twice

D Octopussy

044

James Bond's pistol of choice is a...?

A Walther

B Smith and Wesson

C Luger

D Browning

045

In Goldfinger, Bond crosses swords with the evil Oddjob. Which secret weapon did Oddjob carry?

A A golden gun

B A swordstick

C A boomerang

D A razor-brimmed hat

In The Man With The Golden Gun, Bond has to impersonate the assassin Scaramanga. No easy task as Scaramanga has a rare distinguishing characteristic. What is it?

A He has three nipples

B He has six fingers on each hand

C He has three legs

D He looks like Christopher Lee

James Bond's preferred tipple is...?

A Shandy

B Bourbon

C Gin and tonic

D Vodka martini

Which was the first James Bond film?

A Thunderball

B Dr No

C Goldfinger

D From Russia With Love

049

In From Russia With Love assassin Red Grant impersonates a British agent on a train in order to kill Bond. Fortunately 007 is waiting for him to make his move. What does Grant do to tip Bond off?

Ⓐ Fails to open a door for a lady

Ⓑ Picks his nose

Ⓒ Orders red wine with fish

Ⓓ Claims not to like cricket

050

In License To Kill, Bond finds his friend in a body bag after he has been fed to sharks. There is a note attached to the bag. What does it say?

Ⓐ He suffered a short shark shock

Ⓑ Once bitten, twice shy

Ⓒ Gone fishin'

Ⓓ He disagreed with something that ate him

051

The home of intrepid cartoon superspy Dangermouse is...?

Ⓐ A telephone box

Ⓑ A pillar box

Ⓒ A cardboard box

Ⓓ An exclusive penthouse

His assistant is...?

- **A** Penfold
- **B** Supergran
- **C** Tin Tin
- **D** Domino

Harry Palmer is based on a character in books by Len Deighton. More down-to-earth and much less glamorous than James Bond, he was played on the big screen by...?

- **A** Michael Caine
- **B** Roger Moore
- **C** Dudley Moore
- **D** Orson Welles

Shambolic superspy Austin Powers is played by which actor?

- **A** Gordon Jackson
- **B** Paul Merton
- **C** Patrick McGoohan
- **D** Mike Myers

055 What is the name of the wicked megalomaniac against whom Austin Powers pits his wits?

A Dr Yes

B Dr Kildare

C Dr Mobius

D Dr Evil

056 Robert Vaughn played suave spy Napoleon Solo. For whom did Solo work?

A THRUSH

B MOTHER

C UNCLE

D MI5

057 Where was their secret headquarters?

A Under the river Thames

B Inside a mountain near Geneva

C Behind a secret wall in a New York drycleaners

D Under a Chinese restaurant in Los Angeles

058 What was the name of the character played by Diana Rigg in the cult spy series The Avengers?

A Emma Peel

B Cathy Gale

C Tara King

D Purdey

She was partnered by MI5 undercover agent John Steed, played by Patrick Macnee. What was Steed's weapon of choice?

- **A** Bowler hat and umbrella
- **B** Specially designed catapult
- **C** Purdey 12-bore shotgun
- **D** Browning 9mm

In The Champions, Craig Stirling, Sharron Macready and Richard Barrett worked for a shadowy UN-like organisation called Nemesis. Invariably assigned impossible missions they always managed to save the world. How?

- **A** Each was an expert in their own field
- **B** They were endowed with unbelievable strength and ESP
- **C** They had the very latest gadgets to help them
- **D** They were masters of disguise

How long did the tape recorder that explained the impossible mission at the beginning of Mission Impossible take to self-destruct?

- **A** 5 seconds
- **B** 3 seconds
- **C** 10 seconds
- **D** 30 seconds

062 For whom did the five members of the Mission Impossible team, headed by Jim Phelps, work?

- **A** NATO
- **B** CIA
- **C** MFI
- **D** IMF

063 Who played dashing MI9 agent John Drake in the 1960s hit TV series Danger Man?

- **A** Patrick Macnee
- **B** Patrick McGoohan
- **C** Leslie Howard
- **D** Gordon Jackson

064 Which spy gadget featured in Danger Man was actually used by KGB agents during the Cold War?

- **A** Comb pistol
- **B** Belt buckle radio
- **C** Tiepin camera
- **D** Umbrella sword

065 Who co-starred with Robert Culp in the glossy 1960s spy series I Spy?

- **A** Bill Cosby
- **B** Morgan Freeman
- **C** Sidney Poitier
- **D** Tony Curtis

Intelligence Organisations

What do the letters CIA stand for?

- **A** Central Intelligence Agency
- **B** Criminal Intelligence Agency
- **C** Covert Intelligence Agency
- **D** Clandestine Intelligence Agency

The CIA's headquarters is in...?

- **A** New York
- **B** Washington DC
- **C** Langley, Virginia
- **D** Miami, Florida

A quotation from the Bible is etched into the wall of the CIA's central lobby. What does it say?

- **A** Know the truth and the truth shall set you free
- **B** Do unto others as you would have them do unto you
- **C** Thou shalt not kill
- **D** For truly, there is nothing new under the sun

How many employees does the CIA have?

- **A** 279
- **B** That's classified information
- **C** Around 40,000
- **D** 2000

070

There are more than 70 stars on one wall of the lobby of CIA headquarters. What do they stand for?

A One for every year of the CIA's existence

B Nothing. It's just decoration

C One for every foreign spy arrested and convicted

D One for every CIA agent who died in service of their country

071

Operation Mongoose was the CIA's code name for the elimination of Cuban leader Fidel Castro in the early 1960s. There were at least eight plots to assassinate Castro. Which of the following was not one of them?

A Release a deadly spider in his bedroom

B Give him a box of poisoned or exploding cigars

C Give him a wetsuit contaminated with a poisonous fungus

D Place an exploding seashell near where he liked to scuba dive

072

During the Vietnam war, the CIA and the FBI mounted a joint operation called Operation Chaos to spy on...?

A Americans

B The Russians

C The Vietnamese

D The Chinese

Intelligence Organisations

General Abdul Kassim took power in Iraq after a
bloody coup in 1958. After he renewed diplomatic
relations with the Soviet Union and lifted the ban
on the Iraqi Communist Party, the CIA decided to
assassinate him. What did they use?

    A A sniper

    B Exploding pencil case

    C Poisoned handkerchief

    D Radioactive breakfast cereal

The CIA's secret domestic training base is called...?

    A Camp X-ray

    B School for spies

    C Fort Apache

    D Camp Swampy

Hit by budget cuts and low morale, the CIA has
lost how many of its workforce since the end of
the Cold War?

    A 25%

    B 10%

    C 20%

    D 5%

076

The CIA helped destabilise and overthrow the elected government of which Latin American country after it instituted a program of agrarian reform and confiscated land owned by the US-based United Fruit Company in 1954?

- **A** Haiti
- **B** Guatemala
- **C** Grenada
- **D** El Salvador

077

Which African leader did the CIA target for assassination in 1960?

- **A** Patrice Lumumba
- **B** Idi Amin
- **C** Nelson Mandela
- **D** Haile Selassie

078

What was the name of East Germany's intelligence agency?

- **A** Stampo
- **B** Stasi
- **C** Stolka
- **D** Stoika

Intelligence Organisations

During the Cold War, the East German intelligence service built a huge network of informants and kept files on up to 6 million people — out of a population of only 16 million. Researchers estimate that how many people worked as informers for the Stasi?

A 400,000

B 400

C 40,000

D 4000

The SUPO is the domestic intelligence service of which country?

A Poland

B Mongolia

C Brazil

D Finland

Known as 'the institute' or 'the institution', Mossad is the intelligence agency of which country?

A Israel

B Mozambique

C Norway

D Romania

082

Mossad has a reputation for being one of the world's most effective intelligence agencies. In which year was it formed?

A 1937

B 1951

C 1963

D 1970

083

Mossad is staffed by...?

A Army personnel

B Airforce personnel

C Navy personnel

D Civilians

084

According to leading intelligence experts, how many agents are there in the Kidon, Mossad's assassination squad?

A 10

B About 20

C About 40

D About 130

085

What is or was SMERSH?

A Evil organisation dreamed up by Ian Fleming

B Chinese secret police

C A type of missile

D Assassination division of the KGB

Intelligence Organisations

Which agency is charged with domestic security and counter-intelligence within the United Kingom?

- **A** Scotland Yard
- **B** MI6
- **C** Special Branch
- **D** MI5

086

MI5 is officially known as...?

- **A** The Special Service
- **B** The Security Service
- **C** The Intelligence Service
- **D** The Special Police

087

MI5 has how many staff?

- **A** About 1100
- **B** About 3400
- **C** About 1900
- **D** About 5800

088

The first female director-general of MI5 was...?

- **A** Judi Dench
- **B** Glenda Jackson
- **C** Stella Rimington
- **D** Barbara Castle

089

Intelligence Organisations

090

The foreign section of the British secret service was formed in 1910 under the control of the Admiralty. What was its chief known as?

A Q
B C
C M
D X

091

Despite the dangerous nature of their job an MI6 agent has not officially been killed in action since when?

A First World War
B 1968
C Second World War
D 1984

092

Just as the CIA is informally known internally as 'the Company', MI6 agents also have a name for their agency. What is it?

A The Club
B The Old Boys' Network
C The Team
D The Firm

What is the translation of MI6's Latin motto?

A To find and to know

B To serve the country

C Always secret

D Trust is sacred

How many agents does the FBI have?

A About 5,000

B About 18,000

C About 43,000

D About 28,000

The NBH or National Security Office in English is an intelligence agency in which country?

A Hungary

B Angola

C Costa Rica

D Thailand

The Mubahath el-Dawla or General Directorate of State Security Investigations is the main organisation concerned with domestic security in which country?

A Sudan

B Yemen

C Egypt

D Mauritania

097

In 1900, the Okhrana took over from a succession of secret police organisations in Tsarist Russia. What was its main function?

Ⓐ Monitoring German military strength

Ⓑ Collecting foreign intelligence

Ⓒ Setting up a network of agents in Europe

Ⓓ Monitoring opponents to the Tsar

098

KGB stands for Komitet Gosudarstvennoi Bezopasnosti. What does it mean in English?

Ⓐ Committee for State Security

Ⓑ State Intelligence Agency

Ⓒ Central Security Police

Ⓓ Combined Intelligence Bureau

099

All KGB personnel were issued with uniforms, whether they were plain-clothes operatives or not. What color is associated with the KGB and can be seen on the trim of their uniforms?

Ⓐ Yellow

Ⓑ Red

Ⓒ Green

Ⓓ Blue

Intelligence Organisations

There are four types of intelligence: human intelligence, signals intelligence, satellite intelligence and technical intelligence. During the Cold War, the Western intelligence agencies specialised predominantly in signals and satellite intelligence. What was considered to be the KGB's forte?

- **A** Technical intelligence
- **B** Signals intelligence
- **C** Human intelligence
- **D** Satellite intelligence

According to the KGB's 1967 annual report, how many foreigners did the organisation recruit in that year?

- **A** 3
- **B** 49
- **C** 262
- **D** 218

In the same year, how many double agents planted by the enemy did the KGB discover?

- **A** None
- **B** 172
- **C** 42
- **D** 26

103 How many agents did the KGB plant within their enemies' intelligence services?

- **A** 31
- **B** 58
- **C** 6
- **D** 190

104 The KGB ceased to exist after November of which year?

- **A** 1993
- **B** 1992
- **C** 1991
- **D** 1994

105 Why was the KGB dismantled?

- **A** With the end of the Cold War, it was deemed unnecessary
- **B** Lack of financial resources
- **C** It was involved in an attempted coup
- **D** The CIA requested it

106 What happened to Yevgeny Primakov, the last chairman of the KGB?

- **A** He was arrested, tried and acquitted
- **B** He was tried and sentenced to prison
- **C** He fled to Cuba
- **D** He became the first prime minister of Russia

Intelligence Organisations

The successor to the KGB is the...?

A FSB

B VIP

C FIB

D FDR

This successor suffered from Russia's economic crisis. Meal allowances for employees stopped at the start of 1998 and by September they had only received half their salaries. How many employees did they have in that year?

A 70,000

B 80,000

C 60,000

D 50,000

In 1999, rumors surfaced that the then US president Bill Clinton had been taped having phone sex with Monica Lewinsky by an intelligence agency. Which intelligence agency is alleged to have taped the president?

A MI6

B Mossad

C CIA

D KGB

Intelligence Organisations

110 What is China's intelligence service called?

    A People's Security Service

    B Ministry for State Security

    C Bureau for Domestic Security

    D Chinese Secret Service

111 It is estimated that this organisation keeps individual personnel files on how many urban Chinese?

    A 1 million

    B 400 million

    C 28 million

    D 160 million

112 Which intelligence agency laid off its cleaning staff only to re-employ them at a lower rate in an attempt to slash its budget in the mid-1990s?

    A CIA

    B MI5

    C MI6

    D FBI

113 The Urzad Ochrony Panstwa or UOP is the intelligence agency of which country?

    A Poland

    B Czech Republic

    C Lithuania

    D Kazakhstan

Miscellaneous Spies

Chinese general Sun Tzu mentions spies in his famous treatise on war. He identifies five types of spy: Local spies or inhabitants of the enemy's country; Moles; Double agents; Enemy spies who are allowed to continue unmasked so they can be fed disinformation and Spies who penetrate the enemy's defenses and return with valuable information. When did Sun Tzu write his treatise?

A 1148 AD

B 500 AD

C 500 BC

D 1623 AD

Classified data is...?

A Information available to the general public

B Information organised into specific categories

C A type of computer programme

D Secret information only to be seen by authorized personnel

During the Cold War, most American spies were...?

A White males under 30

B Mainly men between 40 and 50

C An equal mix of men and women

D Of all ages and backgrounds

117

Who is regarded as the founder of modern military espionage?

A Duke of Wellington

B Napoleon Bonaparte

C Cesare Borgia

D Frederick the Great

118

What is the most important task intelligence services and spies perform?

A Assassinations

B Collecting information

C Catching enemy spies

D Destabilising unfriendly regimes

119

Dormant spies placed within an enemy organisation to become active later are called...?

A Sleepers

B Double agents

C Moles

D Badgers

In spy parlance a 'raven' is...?

A A device attached to telephone cables to enable monitoring of conversations

B A type of weapon

C A person under surveillance

D A male agent who seduces women for espionage purposes

The US's first spy network was set up by...?

A George Washington

B Abraham Lincoln

C Woodrow Wilson

D Dwight Eisenhower

The U-2 caused a diplomatic incident in 1960. What type of espionage device was it?

A A robot

B A listening device

C A spy plane

D A tunnel under East Berlin

The U-2 was shot down over the Soviet Union. What was the name of the pilot?

A Gary Powers

B Austin Powers

C Stefanie Powers

D Gary Bonds

124 This pilot carried a poison-tipped needle with which to commit suicide were he captured. Where was it hidden?

- **A** In his watch
- **B** Under a fingernail
- **C** In the heel of his shoe
- **D** Inside a fake dollar coin

125 Rudolph Abel's real name was William Fischer, an undercover Russian spy who entered the US on a forged passport in 1948. He ran a KGB spy ring in New York trying to steal atom bomb secrets. What cover did Fischer use?

- **A** Eccentric artist
- **B** Nuclear physicist
- **C** Milkman
- **D** Business man

126 In Ireland, Spy Wednesday is the Wednesday before...?

- **A** Easter
- **B** Christmas
- **C** St Patrick's Day
- **D** May Day

A missile gap is...?

127

A Difference in the number of missiles one side has over the other

B Positioning of launch sites for optimal efficiency

C Lack of information about enemy missiles

D Separation of the warhead from the rocket body

MI5 kept a file code named 'Henry Worthington' on which political leader?

128

A Neil Kinnock

B Enoch Powell

C Harold Wilson

D Margaret Thatcher

The two major participants in the Cold War were...?

129

A Greenland and Iceland

B USA and China

C Britain and East Germany

D USA and the Soviet Union

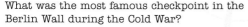

What was the most famous checkpoint in the Berlin Wall during the Cold War?

130

A Checkpoint Boris

B Checkpoint Charlie

C Checkpoint One

D Checkpoint Matilda

Miscellaneous Spies

131

If a secret service operative refers to a 'cobbler', chances are he's referring to...?

- **A** An assassin
- **B** A maker of forged documents
- **C** A getaway driver
- **D** A blackmail attempt

132

The main threat of espionage comes from...?

- **A** Foreign intelligence agencies
- **B** Cleaning staff
- **C** Government employees
- **D** Sophisticated criminals

133

According to Dr Mike Gelles of America's Naval Criminal Investigative Service, most spies...?

- **A** Are highly intelligent
- **B** Are brave and altruistic
- **C** Are greedy
- **D** Suffer from personality disorders

134

A person who helps stop an act of espionage in the USA is eligible for a reward of up to how much?

- **A** $10,000
- **B** $500,000
- **C** $100,000
- **D** $50,000

Miscellaneous Spies

A Chinese employee of an American computer software company resigned his position and took with him software codes with an estimated value of tens of billions of dollars. He was arrested and he confessed, yet walked free from the courtroom. Why?

- **A** The Chinese blackmailed the judge
- **B** The jury were too afraid to convict him
- **C** There was no law against industrial espionage at the time
- **D** Nobody believed his confession

What is a 'floater'?

- **A** A double agent
- **B** A foreign national offering secret information about their country
- **C** Someone used once or only occasionally for an intelligence operation
- **D** A hitman

During the Apartheid regime, South African secret agents tried to assassinate the Reverend Frank Chikane, an opponent of the regime. What did the agents do?

- **A** Mined his garden path
- **B** Gave him an exploding clock
- **C** Poisoned some cheese in his fridge
- **D** Put lethal chemicals in his underpants

Miscellaneous Spies

138 'Hospital' is Russian secret service slang for…?

- **A** Prison
- **B** Moscow
- **C** Debriefing
- **D** Operations in enemy territory

139 Queen Elizabeth I's spymaster was…?

- **A** Sir Francis Walsingham
- **B** Christopher Marlowe
- **C** William Shakespeare
- **D** Sir Francis Drake

140 For an MI5 operative, a 'nugget' is…?

- **A** A surveillance operation
- **B** A mole in a foreign embassy
- **C** False information
- **D** Bait offered to a potential defector

141 A group of British plane-spotters were found guilty in 2002 of espionage in which European country?

- **A** Greece
- **B** France
- **C** Latvia
- **D** Bulgaria

Miscellaneous Spies

Of the Americans arrested for espionage in the USA over the last 50 years, 79%...?

A Spoke with a foreign accent

B Volunteered their services or were recruited by an American friend or relative

C Were in the armed forces

D All of the above

How many were caught by counter-intelligence services before they succeeded in compromising classified material?

A None

B 26%

C 37%

D 48%

A 'wet job' is spy slang for...?

A A covert maritime operation

B A rainy day

C An operation in which blood is spilled

D 24-hour surveillance

145 In 1873 the War Office established an intelligence branch. How many people did it employ?

  A 3
  B Over 400
  C 153
  D 27

146 Which country was thought to have the most elaborate intelligence network in 1900?

  A USA
  B Germany
  C Britain
  D France

147 A female agent used to seduce people for intelligence purposes is known as a...?

  A Swallow
  B Starling
  C Mata Hari
  D Femme fatale

148 A clandestine radio is known as a...?

  A Music box
  B Canary
  C Cell phone
  D Oven

Miscellaneous Spies

In 1953, a delivery boy for the 'Brooklyn Herald' uncovered a Russian spy ring operating in New York. How?

A He was kidnapped by Russian spies but managed to escape

B He saw a man studying secret plans through a window

C He overheard two ladies speaking Russian

D He discovered that a coin he had been given as change was hollow

A person who approaches an intelligence agency with the idea of spying against his or her own country is called a...?

A Trojan horse

B Bearded Jane

C Lure

D Dangle

In 1993, a senior adviser to Boris Yeltsin admitted that Stalin had ordered the assassination of Josep Tito, head of Yugoslavia. With what did Soviet agents plan to kill Tito?

A Poisoned chair

B Poisoned toothbrush

C Poisoned jewel box

D Exploding apple

152 What is Steganography?

    A The science of detecting lies

    B The art of making concealed weapons

    C The practice of writing hidden messages

    D Analysis of satellite images

153 Disinformation played a part in the Cold War when each side tried to undermine the other by planting damaging false rumors in the world's press. The KGB were acknowledged as masters of disinformation which they called 'black propaganda'. Which of the following news stories is not an example of the KGB's black propaganda?

    A Swiss code machines used by many governments around the world had been secretly rigged so the Americans could decipher the messages they sent

    B UN secretary general Dag Hammarskjold was killed by the CIA because he favored too much freedom for African countries

    C The CIA created the AIDS virus as part of a biological warfare program

    D US capitalists kidnapped Latin American babies to sell their body parts for organ transplants

Miscellaneous Spies

What is a 'Black Operation'?

A Covert mission not attributable to the organisation performing it

B Covert mission under cover of darkness

C Covert operation against one of one's own agents

D Bugging one's own headquarters to trap a double agent

The headquarters of an espionage service is known as...?

A Auntie

B Uncle

C Mother

D Father

A relatively small number of traditional spies were killed during the Cold War. "It wasn't gentlemanly, it was just that people didn't kill each other," says David Murphy, a CIA station chief in Berlin for several years. Gathering electronic intelligence however did lead to quite a few casualties. How many US pilots, is it estimated, died on spy missions during the Cold War?

A 150

B 50

C 100

D 200

151

During the Cold War, the CIA dug a long tunnel under the Berlin Wall to tap telephone lines. Unfortunately it turned out to be not the espionage masterstroke that they had planned. What was the problem?

A It wasn't deep enough and was discovered by a group of East German workmen repairing the gas main

B The Russians found the tunnel and flooded it

C They used out-of-date maps of Berlin and the tunnel passed under a long line of disused factories

D A mole in British intelligence told the Russians about it

158

George Blake was a British agent who was recruited by the KGB after he was captured by the North Koreans during the Korean war. How many agents working for the West did Blake give the KGB?

A 100

B 400

C 300

D 200

Miscellaneous Spies

Blake himself was betrayed by a defector from
Polish intelligence. He was sentenced to 42 years
in prison but didn't serve the full term. Why not?

A He died

B He agreed to spy for the West again — to
become a double double agent

C He escaped

D He was pardoned

Which of the following is British Intelligence slang
for a spy?

A Birdwatcher

B Player

C Glider

D Gumshoe

In 1971, a defector gave British intelligence a
list of Russian agents operating in Britain. How
many Soviet intelligence officers did Britain expel
in that year?

A 105

B 82

C 59

D 11

162

A spyglass is another name for what...?

A Magnifying glass

B Binoculars

C Telescope

D Microscope

163

Which of the following isn't considered to be a typical characteristic of a spy engaged in industrial espionage?

A Criminal record

B Military intelligence experience

C 21-35 years old

D Considered an outsider or a loner

164

Convincing yet not critical information fed to a foreign intelligence agency to convince them that a false defector or double agent is genuine is known as...?

A Fish bait

B Chicken feed

C Black gold

D Quicksilver

Miscellaneous Spies

The US developed its atomic bomb at the Los Alamos installation, which was riddled with Soviet spies. Scientists Klaus Fuchs and Ted Hall were just two of the scientists charged with passing secrets to the Russians. In 1949, the Russians tested their own atomic bomb which was remarkably similar to that of the Americans. How much research are the atomic spies estimated to have saved Russia?

A 6 months

B 5 years

C 3 years

D 2 years

An American government study found that 52% of Americans working as spies against the USA ranked what as their primary motivation?

A Money

B Sex

C Need for excitement

D Ideology

Whom of the following was executed after being betrayed by a spy?

A Joan of Arc

B Boudicca

C Christopher Columbus

D Oliver Cromwell

168

Special Branch and MI5 agents are paid...?

A By a secret banker's order

B In gold

C In cash

D By check

169

In which year did the British government formally introduce security vetting for employees occupying sensitive positions?

A 1912

B 1972

C 1960

D 1948

170

When was the German Democratic Republic or East Germany proclaimed?

A 1949

B 1947

C 1941

D 1951

Miscellaneous Spies

Who coined the term 'Iron Curtain' in 1946?

- **A** Roosevelt
- **B** Churchill
- **C** Stalin
- **D** De Gaulle

What is the Increment?

- **A** Elite group of soldiers
- **B** Surveillance satellite
- **C** Covert department within Hungarian intelligence
- **D** Missile guidance system

Which of the following is a spy euphemism for assassination?

- **A** Insider trading
- **B** Executive action
- **C** Boardroom coup
- **D** Managerial meeting

174

What is or was Echelon?

A Global surveillance system

B Code name for Kim Philby

C Encryption machine

D Top secret unit of US Special Forces

175

What is thought to be the most popular method of industrial and personal espionage?

A Encouraging employees or family and friends to 'defect'

B Electronic eavesdropping

C Pretending to be a legitimate visitor or technician

D Rifling through rubbish

176

Which poet and playwright also worked as a secret service spy?

A Christopher Marlowe

B Thomas Kydd

C Cervantes

D William Shakespeare

Mata Hari was the most famous spy of the First World War. Where was she born?

   A Germany

   B Holland

   C France

   D Russia

Matahari is a Malay word that means...?

   A Beautiful but dangerous

   B Dancer

   C Sun behind a cloud

   D Eye of dawn

Between 1905 and 1912, Mata Hari worked as...?

   A Secretary to the French prime minister

   B Policewoman

   C Exotic dancer

   D Bus conductor

180

She was arrested for espionage on 17 Febuary 1917, tried, found guilty and sentenced to death. She was executed on 15 October, by whom?

    A British

    B Germans

    C Americans

    D French

181

Which of the following worked as a spy?

    A David Niven

    B Richard Attenborough

    C Roger Moore

    D Jacques Cousteau

182

Aleksandr Ogorodnik was a high-ranking official in the Soviet Foreign Ministry. Code-named Trigon, he was also a spy for the CIA. In 1977, he was caught taking pictures of secret material and arrested. He agreed to confess but he never went to jail. Why not?

    A The Russians shot him

    B He took a poison pill out of the pen he was using to sign his confession and committed suicide

    C He became a double agent

    D He overpowered his guards, jumped out of the window and escaped

Real Spies

Burgess, Maclean, Philby and Blunt are the most famous British spies of the Cold War. Where did they all meet?

A MCC

B Royal Opera

C Cambridge University

D British Rail waiting room

According to Yuri Moden, the Russian handler for these spies, who was the first of the four to be recruited?

A Blunt

B Maclean

C Burgess

D Philby

Burgess and Maclean joined the Foreign Office. Philby's application was rejected and he worked as a journalist before becoming what?

A A member of Parliament

B An MI6 agent

C Secretary of State for Trade and Industry

D A nightclub owner

186 Philby's real name was Harold Philby. Why was he called Kim?

A His parents had wanted a girl

B It is short for Kimberton, his middle name, which he preferred

C After the boy spy created by Rudyard Kipling

D After the Korean statesman Kim Il Sung, whom he admired

187 In 1951, allied counter-intelligence began to suspect that one of the four was a spy. Which one?

A Philby

B Burgess

C Blunt

D Maclean

188 Philby defected to Russia in 1963. What did he do after that?

A Started a stamp collection

B Was imprisoned

C Continued to work for the KGB

D Became disillusioned and returned to Britain

Anthony Blunt was not publicly unmasked as a Soviet spy until 1979 when he was stripped of his knighthood. When was he actually caught?

A 1975

B 1970

C 1968

D 1964

In Febuary 2001, veteran FBI counter-intelligence agent Robert Hanssen was arrested by the FBI and charged with spying for Russia. What was Hanssen doing at the time of his arrest?

A Placing highly classified material in a dead drop to be picked up by the KGB

B Preparing to flee the country

C Having tea at the Russian embassy

D Watching TV

Markus Wolf was head of international intelligence gathering in the East German secret service for nearly 30 years. What nickname did Western intelligence services give him?

A Goldfinger

B The third man

C The man without a face

D The silver fox

192

Georgi Okolovich was a Russian dissident living in West Germany in the 1950s. The KGB sent Nicolai Kholkhlov, one of their assassins, to kill Okolovich in 1954, but his mission failed. Why?

A The German security forces caught him crossing the border

B Okolovich recognised him and raised the alarm

C He lost his memory

D He converted to Christianity and gave up being an assassin

193

Robert Lipka used to work for America's National Security Agency. In 1996, Lipka was arrested for espionage — 30 years after he left the National Security Agency and 22 years after his last contact with the KGB. How did the FBI catch him?

A His ex-wife went to the authorities

B Found a vital lost clue whilst cleaning out a filing cabinet

C He confessed

D Read a retired KGB general's memoirs and put two and two together

Real Spies

Sidney Reilly was born in 1874. After becoming an international adventurer, fluent in several languages, he began to work for the British secret service. Famous for his courage and indifference to danger, he inspired many books and the TV series Reilly — Ace of Spies where he was played by Sam Neill. Where did Reilly operate?

A China

B France

C South America

D Russia

Virginia Hall, a young American, worked for the French as a spy during the Second World War. She was so successful that the Germans began an all-out hunt for her and were on the point of capturing her in 1941 when she managed to escape on foot over the Pyrenees to Spain. What made her feat all the more remarkable?

A She was wearing high heels

B She was pregnant

C She had a wooden leg

D She was blind

196

Colonel Oleg Penkovsky worked for Soviet Military Intelligence. In 1961, disillusioned with the Soviet system and worried that the world was on the brink of a nuclear war, he volunteered his services to British and American intelligence. Given the code name Hero by the CIA, he provided an astonishing amount of valuable information. However, the information stopped when Penkovsky was arrested by the KGB. How was he caught?

A He had an argument with his wife and she went to the authorities

B He was betrayed by a mole in British intelligence

C He was found with a secret radio

D He was spotted meeting a British contact in Moscow by pure chance

197

In 1986, Vladymir M Ismaylov, a senior Soviet military attache, was expelled from America for activities incompatible with his diplomatic status after being arrested in a remote part of the country. What was Ismaylov doing when he was arrested?

A Electronically eavesdropping on President Reagan who was on holiday at the time

B Taking a cache of microfilm from a carrier pigeon

C Burying money in a milk carton

D Taking pictures of a submarine base

Real Spies

In 1986, Clayton J Lonetree, a US marine and security guard at the US embassy in Moscow and later in Vienna, turned himself in to the authorities. He was arrested, convicted of espionage and sentenced to 30 years in prison after it was found that he had passed classified information to Soviet agents. Why did he do it?

A He fell for a KGB agent

B He was passed over for promotion

C He was paid $1,000,000

D He was bored

Steven J Lalas, a US State Department communications officer, was arrested and charged with passing classified information to a foreign power in 1993. Which foreign power?

A Australia

B Hungary

C Greece

D Russia

In 'Operation Solo', Morris Childs infiltrated and spied on which organisation for the FBI?

A UN

B NATO

C US Communist Party

D KGB

201

Gunter Guillaume was an East German spy trained by the KGB. He entered West Germany as a refugee with instructions to become a West German citizen, find a job and flat and settle down. He became a member of the Social Democratic Party with his wife Christel who was also an East German spy. At some point his handlers activated him and he began to spy for East Germany. He was eventually betrayed by a Soviet defector and arrested. What job did he have when he was arrested in 1974?

A Police inspector

B NATO press secretary

C Counter-intelligence agent

D Personal secretary to the West German chancellor

202

Ursula Kuczynski was one of the most successful female spies in history. A German-born British citizen, she used the alias Ruth Hamburger Beurton and was an important Russian spy during the Second World War and after, passing atomic secrets to Moscow. She fled to East Germany in 1950 and was greeted as a heroine. What was her code name?

A Sonia

B Olga

C Ivana

D Tatiana

Real Spies

Alice Michelson, an East German, was arrested in
New York on 1 October 1984 as she boarded an
aeroplane bound for Czechoslovakia. She was
searched and found to be carrying tape recordings
of classified information. Where had she hidden
the tape recordings?

    A In her hair

    B In a cigarette packet

    C In the heel of her shoe

    D In a false compartment in her
       cell phone

A former Scotland Yard detective sergeant, John
Symonds left Britain in 1969 under suspicion of
corruption. He was approached by foreign agents
in Morocco and recruited by the KGB in Bulgaria.
He was given the code name Scot and specially
trained for undercover missions. What did the
KGB teach him?

    A How to speak nine languages

    B How to be a better lover

    C Conjuring and card tricks

    D Haute cuisine

205

In 1992, KGB librarian Vasili Mitrokhin defected to the West. An MI6 agent went to Russia to smuggle out two huge chests filled with secret KGB files that Mitrokhin had buried near his country cottage. He had smuggled the files out, copied them and returned them. How did he smuggle files out of the heavily-guarded KGB archives?

A Under his hat

B In his shoes

C In a briefcase — he was never searched

D Using a specially trained carrier pigeon

206

One of Mitrokhin's files mentions a British woman, Melita Norwood. Code-named Hola and working as a secretary, she passed scientific and technological secrets to the Soviets for over 40 years, including top secret information on the atomic bomb. She wasn't unmasked until 1992 when Mitrokhin's files were analysed. What is she doing now?

A Serving a 27-year prison sentence

B Living in political asylum in Moscow

C Living in hiding somewhere, probably in the Balkans

D Living quietly in South London and making jam

Passwords used to identify secret agents to one another are called...?

A Cloaks

B Letters

C Paroles

D Keys

In intelligence circles, a false passport or visa is referred to as a...?

A Shoe

B String vest

C Blag

D Bouncing Czech

In 1994, Aldrich Ames was arrested and sentenced to life imprisonment without parole for selling secrets to the KGB. During his time as a mole, for whom did Ames work?

A MI5

B FBI

C CIA

D Pentagon

210 Within the space of a decade, he revealed more than 100 covert operations and betrayed...?

- **A** 10 agents
- **B** 40 agents
- **C** 20 agents
- **D** 30 agents

211 How many of the double agents exposed by Ames managed to escape alive?

- **A** One
- **B** Five
- **C** Two
- **D** None

212 Why did he say he did it?

- **A** He enjoyed the excitement
- **B** Disillusionment with the CIA
- **C** He was a communist
- **D** Greed

Spycraft – what every spy should know

You're on the trail of an evil master spy and all you have to go on is the name of a girlfriend he had when he was 20. You need to find her and talk to her. Women are more difficult to trace than men because...?

- **A** They often dye their hair
- **B** They may change their surname if they marry
- **C** They sometimes lie about their age
- **D** They are more suspicious than men

Which of the following may not be a sign that someone has sent you a bomb?

- **A** Handwritten address
- **B** Wires protruding from the package
- **C** No stamps or non-franked stamps
- **D** Wrapped in string

You are being pursued by trackers with dogs. Rushing through the woods, you come to a shallow river. What do you do?

- **A** Keep going in a straight line
- **B** Climb a tree
- **C** Submerge yourself under a lily pad and breathe through a reed
- **D** Follow the river, criss-crossing it

216

If you are being pursued by tracker dogs, the best thing you can do is drop something to destroy their sense of smell. What should you use if tracked by bloodhounds?

A Cayenne pepper

B Salt

C Fresh meat

D Ammonia

217

And if you are pursued by German Shepherds who sniff air rather than the ground?

A Fresh meat

B Cayenne pepper

C Ammonia

D Salt

218

The simplest invisible inks are organic compounds which are invisible at room temperature but which turn brown when heated. Which of the following can't be used to make invisible ink?

A Salt water

B Vinegar

C Lemon juice

D Urine

Spycraft – what every spy should know

How far away can you generally hear a rifle shot at night?

- **A** 5 miles
- **B** Half a mile
- **C** 400 yards
- **D** One and half miles

How far away can you see the light from a match or cigarette on a clear night?

- **A** Half a mile
- **B** 100 yards
- **C** A mile
- **D** 10 yards

How long does it take the eyes to develop 'night vision'?

- **A** 60 minutes
- **B** 15 minutes
- **C** 30 minutes
- **D** 5 minutes

Lack of which vitamin reduces night vision?

- **A** Vitamin A
- **B** Vitamin B
- **C** Vitamin C
- **D** Vitamin D

223

If you are on a night mission, using a light may give your position away. However, if you need light and are in a secure position you can use a filtered light to avoid ruining your night vision. Which color filter should you use?

A Blue

B Green

C Red

D White

224

Darkness distorts vision, modifying outlines, distances and color. Generally, visual sharpness at night is…?

A One third of what it is during the day

B One quarter of what it is during the day

C One tenth of what it is during the day

D One seventh of what it is during the day

225

If you are going to fire a machine gun at night, what shouldn't you do?

A Keep one eye closed

B Fire slightly above the target

C Make sure there's a bullet in the chamber first

D Fire short bursts

Spycraft – what every spy should know

The most accurate and efficient way to fire a pistol is...?

A Sitting down

B Using a two-handed grip

C Firing from the hip

D Resting the barrel on your forearm

In combat or on the run, pistols are generally deadly at a range of...?

A Up to 10 meters

B Up to 50 meters

C Up to 25 meters

D Up to 100 meters

You've stolen some secret plans and the enemy is scouring the area looking for you. You are hiding in some undergrowth when you spot an enemy patrol heading straight for you. What do you do?

A Run for it

B Stay cool and don't move

C Attack them

D Move away very slowly

229

You're breaking into the heavily guarded castle of a criminal mastermind to steal some secret papers when you are confronted by a large guard dog. The dog springs for your throat but you manage to protect yourself with your forearm. The dog sinks its teeth into your arm. You need to free yourself before the dog does any serious damage and before its handler arrives. What do you do?

A Look it in the eyes and try and hypnotise it

B Grab its windpipe and squeeze until it loses consciousness

C Try and pull its front legs apart

D Tell it to let go in a firm voice

230

You are seconded to counter-intelligence to conduct surveillance on a suspected spy. You'll need a car from the motor pool. Which should you choose?

A Jaguar E type — you've always wanted to drive one

B Ferrari — you never know when you'll need to put your foot down

C Ford Escort — homely but inconspicuous

D Rolls Royce — might as well make yourself as comfortable as possible for a long day

Spycraft – what every spy should know

Whenever you leave your car unattended, you always place a small compass in it. Why?

A You were in the scouts

B No reason, it's just a foible

C It will tell you if someone has bugged or bombed your car

D You like to know which direction you're heading

To conduct a surveillance operation from a vehicle, what do you need?

A Video camera

B High-resolution camera

C Packed lunch

D All of the above

You follow a double agent to his rendezvous with his controller on a deserted beach. The nearest cover is over 100 yards from the spies and the sound of the surf covers their speech when you try and use the listening device you brought along. What else can you use to listen in?

A Binoculars

B Pistol

C Nothing

D Ear trumpet

234

You've photographed a secret message using a high resolution camera but how do you make it into a microdot?

- **A** Develop the film, light the negative from behind and photograph it again. Cut out the bit you want from the second negative
- **B** Fold the film up very small
- **C** Put it in the wash so it shrinks
- **D** You can't. You need a special miniature camera

235

You've been picked up by the police whilst on assignment in a distant foreign land. As far as you know, your cover hasn't been blown, but they are suspicious of you. You've been reasonably well-treated so far. The interrogator seems fair and polite. After some routine questions, he asks if you will consent to a polygraph, or lie-detector test. What do you do?

- **A** Confess immediately. They'll go easy on you if you co-operate
- **B** Refuse to take a polygraph
- **C** Overpower the interrogator and escape
- **D** Agree. You know you can deceive the polygraph

Spycraft – what every spy should know

You can beat a polygraph by...?

A Controlling your breathing

B Tensing your legs

C Answering all the questions falsely

D Refusing to answer any questions

236

As well as controlling your breathing, you need to control your heart rate and blood pressure. Which of the following techniques can't you use to do this during a polygraph test?

A Contracting your sphincter muscle

B Lightly biting your tongue

C Thinking exciting thoughts

D Pressing your feet into the floor

237

If you are being interrogated, you should...?

A Pretend to be mad

B Show no emotion

C Ask for food and drink

D Act natural

238

Which of the following makes the best secret agent?

A Light drinker

B Heavy drinker

C Social drinker but able to handle it

D Teetotaler

239

240

A polygraph is basically a combination of medical devices designed to monitor changes occurring in the body. Which of the following doesn't the polygraph monitor?

A Respiratory rate

B Blood pressure

C Electro-dermal activity

D Pupil dilation

241

You are on a surveillance assignment.
You have followed the target back to his home where you're pretty sure he will stay until tomorrow morning. You're due to be relieved at midnight and you keep watch on the target's home until then. A small boy walks down the street with a puppy. Suddenly, a black car screeches to a halt and a huge, dangerous-looking man jumps out. He starts punching and kicking the boy and the puppy. There aren't many people about and they pretend not to see what is happening. What do you do?

A Ring the police

B Nothing

C Take a second or two to definitively resolve the situation using your martial arts skills

D Try to talk to the attacker and calm him down

Spycraft – what every spy should know

Which martial art is favored by the Israeli armed forces?

- **A** Krav Maga
- **B** Judo
- **C** Karate
- **D** Aikido

The magazine of which assault rifle makes an excellent can and bottle opener?

- **A** Galil
- **B** Kalashnikov
- **C** Armalite
- **D** M16

You're walking down a busy high street shadowing a foreign spy at a discreet distance. Suddenly, your target turns right into what you know is a dead end. What does this mean?

- **A** He's leaving information at a dead drop
- **B** He's lost
- **C** There must be a secret door somewhere
- **D** He suspects he's being followed

245

You can make a lockpick out of which of the following?

Ⓐ Bicycle spokes

Ⓑ Bristles from a roadsweeper's brush

Ⓒ Nails

Ⓓ All of the above

246

Karate originated on the Japanese island of Okinawa. What does karate mean?

Ⓐ Take that

Ⓑ Solid wall

Ⓒ Empty hand

Ⓓ Punch and kick

247

In self-defense terms, what does the acronym TEK stand for...?

Ⓐ Thwart Every Kick

Ⓑ Timing, Energy, Kinetics

Ⓒ Throat, Eyes, Knees

Ⓓ Train, Endure, Knock out

You're on your way home, your mission completed. Unfortunately the enemy have got wind of you and are in hot pursuit. They haven't had time to seal the border but they do have a henchman blocking the road in front of you. You'll have to bust through the roadblock. Which part of the henchman's car do you aim at?

A The rear

B The middle

C The front

D Makes no difference

When given the option, it is better to avoid rather than try to break through roadblocks. On being confronted with a roadblock, one technique you can use is the bootleg turn or 180 degree turn. Maintain your speed, disengage the clutch and turn the wheel from 12 o'clock to 6 o'clock with one hand whilst simultaneously engaging the handbrake with the other. The car will start to spin in the direction you turn the wheel. At what point should you disengage the handbrake and return the wheel to 12 o'clock?

A When you've turned 90 degrees

B Immediately

C When you've turned 180 degrees

D When you get dizzy

250

Another technique is the j-turn or reverse 180. What advantage does the j-turn have over the bootleg turn?

A It's easier to execute

B It requires less space between you and the roadblock

C It's faster

D It looks more spectacular

251

You're driving along when the opposition pulls up alongside you and point a gun at you. What should you do?

A Brake suddenly

B Surrender

C Accelerate away

D Ram them

252

What is the 'Stockholm Syndrome'?

A A spy film starring Britt Ekland

B The theory of mutually assured destruction in the event of a nuclear war between East and West

C The theory that there is a mole in every intelligence organisation

D The tendency of hostages to identify with their captors

Spycraft – what every spy should know

You're carrying out a surveillance operation in New York when you intercept a police radio transmission. The dispatcher tells a patrol car to respond to a code 905N and gives the address you're watching. Do you make a hasty getaway or not? What is a code 905N?

- **A** Jail break
- **B** Noisy animal
- **C** Burglar alarm ringing
- **D** Person with a gun

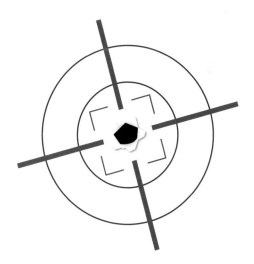

Case Studies

Imagine for a moment that you are CIA counter-intelligence chief James Angleton. The year is 1964. John F Kennedy was assassinated last year. The Cold War is raging all around the globe. The air is thick with fear, tension and paranoia. KGB officer Yuri Nosenko has just defected to the West. According to Nosenko he led the KGB's investigation of Lee Harvey Oswald after Kennedy's assassination and he has information for you. His story raises suspicions in your office. Some of your agents think that the KGB have sent Nosenko to dispel rumors of Soviet involvement in Kennedy's death. Some of the information he has provided contradicts intelligence given by Anatoly Golitsyn, a previous defector. Golitsyn has long warned that the KGB would send false defectors to discredit his assertion that the Russians have a mole inside the CIA. If Nosenko is a genuine defector he could provide valuable information. If not, he could use disinformation to impede the hunt for the mole or he might even be a double agent. It seems too much of a coincidence that Oswald's case offer should defect right after the assassination but would the Russians really be so clumsy and transparent? What are you going to do?

- **A** Believe Golitsyn and treat Nosenko as a false defector

- **B** Believe Nosenko. Treat his information as good and keep Golitsyn under surveillance

- **C** Treat both Golitsyn and Nosenko as suspicious and to investigate them both

- **D** Do nothing. Wait and see what happens

The year is 1982. It appears the KGB have obtained information that could only have come from within a top secret research institute. You are a British counter-intelligence agent who has been called in to investigate. You don't have any hard evidence to go on but it seems that the security breach has originated from within a group of four employees. You begin your investigation with a review of their personnel files. Who arouses your suspicions the most?

File A

Name: Gary Warner

Title: Systems analyst

Gender: Male

Age: 41

Place of Birth: Brentwood, Essex

Marital status: Married to Anne, a nurse, for 16 years. Four children: David (14), Susan (12), Liam (9) and Russell (2)

Education: BSc Computer Science Hull University

Income: £20,000 annual salary

Finances: Co-owns £82,000 house with Susan. £60,000 mortgage more or less up to date. Took out £10,000 personal loan 3 years ago. Repaid in full 5 months ago. Credit card debt of £1280

Background: Oldest of two children. Father worked in local car factory before being made redundant two years ago. Mother took part-time job in supermarket to help with family finances

Interests: Avid soccer fan who travels to matches whenever possible. Last year began attending meetings of extreme right wing organisations

Investigator's comments: Highly competent at his job but co-workers regard him as arrogant and aloof. Was given a verbal warning for poor timekeeping last year and rebuked for poor work and a refusal to follow proper procedure 8 months ago. His latest performance review was very positive

File B

Name: John Wright

Title: Physicist (houseman)

Gender: Male

Age: 23

Place of Birth: Swindon, Wiltshire

Marital status: Single, occasional light relationships

Education: BSc Physics Cambridge University, MSc Particle Physics Cambridge University. Currently studying for a PhD also at Cambridge University

Income: £10,000 annual fellowship. Parents and student grants help with living expenses

Finances: Rents a small flat for £120 per month. Rent is sometimes paid a few days late. £135 credit card debt

Background: Youngest of three children. Parents live in Swindon. Father is a civil engineer with a large construction company, mother is a housewife. Mother sent two letters to The Times protesting about the war in Vietnam. As a schoolboy, he wrote an article in the school paper protesting about the blockade of Cuba

Interests: Builds electronic gadgets in his spare time. Chess grandmaster. Was involved in leftwing politics at university. Attended Communist Party meetings but did not join

Investigator's comments: He is a scientific prodigy who was awarded a First Class Honors Degree at the age of 18. An enthusiastic and committed worker with a genuine gift for Physics, he is a highly valued employee of the institute

File C

Name: James Endsleigh-White

Title: Project co-ordinator

Gender: Male

Age: 48

Place of Birth: Little Whittington, Surrey

Marital status: Married to Georgina for 26 years. No children. Wife heads various local charitable associations and societies

Education: BSc Chemical Engineering Oxford University, MBA Harvard Business School

Income: £56000 annual salary plus income from various stocks and shares options

Finances: Lives in a large townhouse valued at £285,000 which he owns outright. Also owns a small flat in London and an estate in Cheshire inherited from his late father

Background: Only child. Father was a wealthy industrialist. Mother was a society hostess

Interests: Collects rare books. Chairman of local cricket club

Investigator's comments: Well-liked by colleagues but rarely socialises with workmates and keeps himself to himself. Unsubstantiated rumors of an affair with a young actress several years ago

File D

Name: Elisabeth Wilhelm

Title: Chemical engineer

Case Studies

Gender: Female

Age: 34

Place of Birth: East Berlin, German Democratic Republic

Marital status: Married to Klaus Wilhelm, owner of a graphic design company. No children

Education: BSc Chemistry Nottingham University

Income: £28,000 annual salary

Finances: Co-owns house with husband. Valued at £115000. Mortgage £72000. Payments up to date. £690 credit card debt

Background: Oldest of four children she emigrated from East Berlin with her parents as a child. Has many relatives in East Germany. Father is a retired plumber. Mother is a retired postwoman

Interests: Avid theater and cinema-goer. Attends creative writing classes at local college

Investigator's comments: Solid, conscientious worker with a positive attitude

A File A: Gary Warner

B File B: John Wright

C File C: James Endsleigh-White

D File D: Elisabeth Wilhelm